EXPECTATIONS

Five Addresses for Those Beginning Ministry

Sister Edmée SLG

SLG Press
Convent of the Incarnation
Fairacres Oxford

ISBN 0 7283 0147 4
ISSN 0307 – 1405

Printed and Bound by Will Print, Oxford, England

ACKNOWLEDGEMENTS

We are grateful to the following publishers for permission to quote from published works: HarperCollins Publishers, *Purity of Heart is to Will One Thing* by Søren Kierkegaard, and *The Silver Chair* by C. S. Lewis; Oxford University Press, NY, *The Idea of the Holy* by Rudolf Otto.

CONTENTS

PREFACE

These addresses were first given to the Lincoln College Leavers' Retreat, 5-7 May 1986, and the last three, on Poverty, Chastity and Obedience, were also given to Westcott House, 11-12 December 1988, plus an addition on the 'tunics of skin' to the address on Obedience. Eleven years later we have finally succeeded in preparing them for publication, other demands on SLG Press and other pursuits on my part continually having intervened to prevent the necessary work being done on them earlier. The decision in the meanwhile of the Church of England to ordain women to the priesthood has also necessitated some adjustments, though no alteration of substance, because from the start the addresses were conceived with the spiritual life of the priest in mind.

In the first two addresses, 'Thanksgiving', and 'Expectations', the immediate concerns of those beginning ministry remained uppermost in my thinking, but in the application of the Evangelical Counsels of Poverty, Chastity and Obedience to the priestly life I aimed high, in the spirit of George Herbert, from whose prelude to *The Country Parson* I quote at the beginning of the addresses on Poverty. It may seem to some that I aimed too high. But those called to the priestly dignity will always desire 'a mark to aim at,' as Herbert says, and I hope some will find in these addresses just such an aim.

Sister Edmée SLG
Fairacres
Feast of St Peter and St Paul 1997

I

THANKSGIVING

Almighty and everlasting God,
you are always more ready to hear than we to pray
and give more than either we desire or deserve.
Pour down upon us the abundance of your mercy,
forgiving us those things of which our conscience is afraid
and giving us those good things which we are not worthy to ask
save through the merits and mediation
of Jesus Christ your Son our Lord.

ASB Collect for Easter V

It would be hard to find a more appropriate collect for the beginning of a retreat: 'You are always more ready to hear than we to pray.' Of all the collects it is the one which has moved me most since I first came to know it. It at once conjures up the picture—anthropomorphic certainly, but I shall not be talked out of it on that account—of God sitting in heaven, leaning over, a hand cupped to his ear and an expression of yearning on his face as he longs for me to stop and pray to him; he who waits only for the first sign of prayer from me to give me more than I dare to desire and never can deserve; to pour down upon me the abundance of his mercy; to forgive me those things which burden my conscience; and to give me those good things of which only the indwelling of him into whose Body I have been incorporated by baptism can make me worthy.

Dr Goulburn, whose magisterial two-volume work on the Prayer Book Collects, first published in 1880 and never surpassed, confirms the picture I get from the prayer by tracing to Gelasius a thought in it, now lost, which, Goulburn says, calls to mind the parable of the Prodigal Son. This is what he tells us of the collect's history:

1

The first draft of it is found in the earliest of the Sacramentaries, that of Leo. Gelasius, without materially altering the sentiment, recast the language, and expanded it a little at the end. Cranmer inserted in the earlier part a clause which was not there before... As Gelasius left the collect it opened thus: 'Almighty God, who in the abundance of thy fatherly compassion dost surpass both the desires and deserts of those who pray to thee.' Cranmer dropped the expression 'in the abundance of thy fatherly compassion,' and substituted for it this definite statement of the way in which God's fatherly compassion manifests itself, 'who art always more ready to hear than we to pray.'[1]

How Cranmer's genius is revealed in that marvellous stroke! But Goulburn regrets the loss of 'in the abundance of thy fatherly compassion' for he goes on:

The two expressions together [namely, 'in the abundance of thy fatherly compassion' and 'who art always more ready to hear than we to pray'], neither of which we can well afford to lose, irresistibly call to mind the Parable of the Prodigal Son.[2]

By suggesting to us the parable of the Prodigal Son, Goulburn's account of the collect recalls to us the beginning of our own pilgrimage. Was there not a moment—perhaps many such moments—when we came to ourselves in our personal pigsties and suddenly understood our situation? I think this happens to all of us in different ways and from different points of departure. It may seem that some pigsties are in more of a mess than others, but from the point of view of the soul it is all the same whether it comes to itself in a den of iniquity or in a bright parlour in some respectable semi-detached. We all know, either intuitively or through sheer experience, what it means to waste the substance of our soul, and the sense of impoverishment which follows. But if that sense of impoverishment has brought us to penitence, what

---

[1] *The Collects of the Day*, Vol. II, pp. 89–90.
[2] Ibid., p. 90.

joy there has been in seeing the Father hastening towards us! What comfort we have known in the love which is ready to embrace us while we are still far off! And with what longing we look forward to being clothed in a robe of glory and to receiving the ring which will seal our eternal union with him! Meanwhile, during the years of our return, and the difficulties of the way back—about which the parable is silent—we make discoveries which are crucial to our perseverance. We find that 'in everything God works for good with those who love him.' And so our collect leads us into that great passage from Romans 8:28–end, the whole of which speaks to us 'who are called according to his purpose.' In his commentary on this passage in *The Epistle of Paul to the Romans*, C. H. Dodd is anxious we should note that Paul's promise of God's co-operation 'with those who love him' is immediately substituted by 'who are called according to his purpose' so that we may avoid the conclusion that it is by our love for God that we have merited his co-operation. Dodd goes on to quote from Rudolph Otto's, *The Idea of the Holy*:

> The idea of 'election'—i.e., of having been chosen and pre-ordained by God *unto salvation*—is an immediate and pure expression of the actual religious experience of grace. The recipient of divine grace feels and knows ever more and more surely, as he looks back on his past, that he has not grown into his present self through any achievement or effort of his own, and that, apart from his own will or power, grace was imparted to him, grasped him, impelled, and led him. And even the resolves and decisions that were most his own and most free become to him, without losing the element of freedom, something that he *experienced* rather than *did*. Before every deed of his own he sees love the deliverer in action, seeking and selecting, and acknowledges that an eternal gracious purpose is watching over his life.[3]

---

[3] OUP, London, 1923, p. 87. I have used this translation in preference to Dodd's translation of the passage.

This eternal gracious purpose we can call providence, and there is not one of you who cannot have recognised a marvellous providence at work in your life or you would not be here, though some probably recognise it more readily than others. But whether you recognise it much or little, the importance of giving heartfelt thanks for whatever you do see of it cannot be overestimated, for providence, once it has chosen us—for reasons which grow ever more mysterious as we grow in self-knowledge—increases its activity in our lives in direct proportion to our response to it.

This response, which is itself the work of grace, sooner or later brings us to a moment when suddenly we see the entire tapestry of our life as being of a piece, transfigured, as it were, so that not just the 'good' things but all the 'bad' things are seen to be equally part of the design, equally necessary for the ultimate completion of the picture. And when this moment comes we can even weep tears of gratitude for the most painful and adverse circumstances, as for example, what we had thought were awful parents, a wretched and deprived childhood, or an innate lack of capacity in some direction or other in ourselves which has been a source of endless unhappiness. All such causes of grief and frustration and resentment are revealed in rare moments of exaltation as having been prepared uniquely for us; as having been precisely, to the millionth of an inch, what was required in our particular case if we were, and are, to grow to the 'measure of the stature of the fullness of Christ' (Eph. 4:13).

> Then Joseph could refrain himself no longer... And he wept aloud, and the Egyptians and the household of Pharaoh heard it... And he said, 'I am your brother, Joseph, whom you sold into Egypt. And now do not be distressed, or angry with yourselves, because you sold me here; for God sent me before you to preserve life... God sent me before you to preserve for you a remnant on earth, to keep alive for you many survivors. So it was not you who sent me here, but God. And he has made me

4

a father to Pharaoh, and lord of all his house and ruler over all the land of Egypt. Gen. 45:1ff.

In Joseph we are given an example of spiritual stature established in such fullness that he is shown responding not to the iniquities of human nature but only to the workings of divine providence. And so divine providence makes him a 'father to Pharaoh, lord of all his house, and ruler over all the land of Egypt.' Moreover, the exaltation of mind which caused him to weep aloud when he made himself known to his treacherous brothers, and to embrace them with a love requiring no element of forgiveness because for him no injury had been done, was not a passing state he was unable to sustain but an abiding disposition, as is made clear five chapters later when, after the death of their father, the brothers send a messenger to Joseph:

> Your father gave this command before he died, 'Say to Joseph, Forgive, I pray you, the transgression of your brothers and their sin, because they did evil to you.' And now, we pray you, forgive the transgression of the servants of the God of your father. Joseph wept when they spoke to him [and said] 'Fear not, for am I in the place of God? As for you, you meant evil against me; but God meant it for good, to bring about that many people should be kept alive, as they are today.
> Gen. 50:15ff.

What is striking here is that Joseph again weeps, this time at the moment of being asked to forgive the transgression of his brothers, which suggests to my mind that he is shown to be moved not because they are his brothers—though their relationship to him is a significant aspect of the story—but because they once again recall themselves to him as instruments of God's providence.

So we may take Joseph as being a model of that magnanimity which springs from an intimate relationship with God; one who experienced to the full that God works for good with those whom he has called according to his purpose. We, on the other hand—and I speak from long experience of myself—may be more like the brothers whose fears of an alteration in Joseph's state were based on the expectations they would have had of themselves had the positions been reversed. In most of us the flame of resentment is not easily extinguished but remains, however well turned down, ready to flare up at unexpected moments, sometimes many years after we had thought ourselves freed from whatever the source of it may have been.

And that we are like this we must patiently accept because unlike Joseph we are not unified in ourselves, and so we will feel one thing at one time and something else at another. But one of the shortest routes to unification is thanksgiving: thanksgiving of the kind which moves us to tears of penitence and joyful humility. Thanksgiving to him whose assurance we know to be true: that the very hairs of our head are all numbered.

And so I should like to suggest that you spend the first few hours of the retreat looking back over your spiritual journey, giving thanks for all the people who have played a part in it, and for all those circumstances which have mysteriously worked together for your good. To adapt the words of a Holy Week collect: enter with joy upon the meditation of those mighty acts in your own life whereby you have been given life and immortality.

*　　*　　*　　*　　*

II

EXPECTATIONS

In our first address we thought about providence, about how God works for good with those whom he has called according to his purpose, and we looked back with thanksgiving over all the people and circumstances which have contributed to the progress of our spiritual journey so far. Such looking back lays a foundation of trust in God for the future —and trust in God is what anyone setting out on the path of priesthood will need above all else. In this talk we will think about the spirit in which we are approaching the future, and in particular we will think about our expectations.

Expectations! What a terrible curse our expectations are! Is it too much to say that they can ruin our lives? Yes, perhaps it is. At least, it is too much to say of us for it is unlikely that any of us would be together in this place if we had not shown signs along the line of being able to adapt our expectations to reality. You will all, for instance, have had expectations about your theological college which doubtless underwent swift modifications within days of your entry into it; likewise expectations about the qualities essential in an ordinand to the sacred ministry which, at first sight, none of your fellow ordinands appeared to be within miles of possessing!

But what about all those expectations, conscious and unconscious, which have been forming in each of you about life in the parish? These are the ones which are going to matter, the ones which could make life very difficult for you, and the ones which could hinder your proclamation of the Gospel. One of the dangers I am envisaging is portrayed in C. S. Lewis's Narnia story, *The Silver Chair*. Let us enter that enchanted world.

Two children, Jill Pole and Eustace Scrubb, are drawn into the world of Narnia by a noble lion called Aslan, a symbolic figure whose meaning becomes clear as the story proceeds. Aslan gives the children the task of finding the lost prince of Narnia who has been bewitched by a beautiful sorceress, and he instructs Jill in four signs that she must learn by heart, repeat night and morning, and act upon as soon as they are encountered. At an early stage in their quest they meet a Marsh-wiggle called Puddleglum whose expectations about everything are wonderfully and profoundly gloom-filled. To Jill's relief he agrees to join them, saying:

> 'I'll come with you, sure and certain. I'm not going to lose an opportunity like this. It will do me good. They all say—I mean, the other wiggles all say—that I'm too flighty; don't take life seriously enough. If they've said it once, they've said it a thousand times. "Puddleglum," they've said, 'you're altogether too full of bobance and bounce and high spirits. You've got to learn that life isn't all fricasseed frogs and eel pie. You want something to sober you down a bit. We're only saying it for your own good, Puddleglum." That's what they say. Now a job like this—a journey up north just as winter's beginning, looking for a Prince that probably isn't there, by way of a ruined city that no one has ever seen—will be just the thing. If that doesn't steady a chap, I don't know what will.' And he rubbed his big frog-like hands together as if he were talking of going to a party or a pantomime.[4]

So they set out in search of the City Ruinous, and their way is long and perilous, cold and comfortless. But they make good progress and succeed in passing the horrible giants of Ettinsmoor without being noticed. Then they come upon an ancient giant road stretching away before them into the heart of the mountains, and riding towards them are two people, one a knight in complete armour with his visor down, and the other a lovely lady riding on a white horse.

---

[4] Puffin Books, 1965, p. 70. (First published in Penguin Books, 1953).

'Good day, travellers,' she cried out in a voice as sweet as the sweetest bird's song... 'Some of you are young pilgrims to walk this rough waste.' 'That's as may be, Ma'am,' said Puddleglum very stiffly and on his guard. 'We're looking for the ruined city of the giants,' said Jill. 'The ruined city?' said the Lady. 'That is a strange place to be seeking. What will you do if you find it?' 'We've got to—' began Jill, but Puddleglum interrupted. 'Begging your pardon, Ma'am. But we don't know you or your friend—a silent chap, isn't he?—and you don't know us. And we'd as soon not talk to strangers about our business, if you don't mind. Shall we have a little rain soon, do you think?'

The Lady laughed: the richest, most musical laugh you can imagine. 'Well, children,' she said, 'you have a wise, solemn old guide with you. I think none the worse of him for keeping his own counsel, but I'll be free with mine. I have often heard the name of the giantish City Ruinous, but never met any who would tell me the way thither. This road leads to the burgh and castle of Harfang, where dwell the gentle giants. They are as mild, civil, prudent, and courteous as those of Ettinsmoor are foolish, fierce, savage, and given to all beastliness. And in Harfang you may or may not hear tidings of the City Ruinous, but certainly you shall find good lodgings and merry hosts. You would be wise to winter there, or, at the least, to tarry certain days for your ease and refreshment. There you shall have steaming baths, soft beds, and bright hearths; and the roast and the baked and the sweet and the strong will be on the table four times in a day.' 'I say!' exclaimed Scrubb. 'That's something like! Think of sleeping in a bed again.' 'Yes, and having a hot bath,' said Jill. 'Do you think they'll ask us to stay? We don't know them, you see.' 'Only tell them,' answered the Lady, 'that She of the Green Kirtle salutes them by you, and has sent two fair Southern children for the Autumn Feast.'[5]

The Knight and the Lady go on their way, and now they nearly have the first of the quarrels which Puddleglum had foretold. Puddleglum doesn't want them to go to Harfang at all, reminding them that Aslan's signs said nothing about

---

[5] Ibid pp. 79ff

staying with giants, gentle or otherwise. The children, however, are absolutely dead set on visiting the Gentle Giants, and in the end Puddleglum gives in. The story continues:

> After that talk with the Lady things got worse in two different ways. In the first place the country was much harder. The road led through endless, narrow valleys down which a cruel north wind was always blowing in their faces. There was nothing that could be used for firewood, and there were no nice little hollows to camp in...
>
> In the second place, whatever the Lady had intended by telling them about Harfang, the actual effect on the children was a bad one. They could think about nothing but beds and baths and hot meals and how lovely it would be to get indoors. They never talked about Aslan, or even about the lost prince, now. And Jill gave up her habit of repeating the signs over to herself every night and morning. She said to herself, at first, that she was too tired, but she soon forgot all about it. And though you might have expected that the idea of having a good time at Harfang would have made them more cheerful, it really made them more sorry for themselves and more grumpy and snappy with each other and with Puddleglum.[6]

Well, the result is that they miss the next sign and duly arrive at Harfang where they are welcomed by the giants, given hot baths, soft beds and scrumptious food. But the comforts of the place take on a different light when they discover, from reading a recipe book left open on the kitchen table at instructions for making a 'Man Pie', that the giants are planning to eat them at their Autumn Feast only two days away. Of course, they escape, and with enormous difficulty get back on to the right track. Eventually they rescue the prince from the beautiful witch, and the book ends with the triumph of good over evil—which is only right and proper in a story which is intended to be an allegory of the Christian life.

---

[6] Ibid., pp. 83ff.

The character of Puddleglum is worth pondering. I think he represents that element in us which, if we make a friend of it and stop to listen to its unwelcome warnings, will keep us close to the facts, to that reality of which Eliot rightly said, human beings cannot stand very much. But being a Puddleglum, in the way Lewis presents the character, is not to be confused with merely reacting negatively to whatever is said, or to whatever happens—about which there is nothing to be said in favour. No, Puddleglum, I think, is one who looks at a situation until he has seen the cross in it, and then he goes into it—much like the apostle Thomas whose response to Jesus' intention to go to Lazarus is to say: 'Let us also go, that we may die with him' (John 11:16).

Now whether your expectations of life in the parish—or wherever it is you are going—will be fulfilled or disappointed will depend largely on the spirit in which you committed yourself. If like Puddleglum you looked the adventure full in the face and said to yourself, 'Now a job like this—a journey up north just as winter's beginning...' then the chances are that all will be well with you, for you will have glimpsed and accepted the inevitable cross in the situation. But if you were seduced by the thought of hot baths and soft beds, then it is possible that your way will be made much harder. Only your personal self-examination can reveal which of these attitudes belonged to you at the time of making the decision. But, even if you are forced to admit that the latter is nearer the mark, all is not lost! 'A broken and a contrite heart, God will not despise!' For if one suspects that one's motives have been coloured by self-interest, vanity, or ambition, and one allows the suspicion to emerge into the light of day, acknowledging it with all simplicity, then something mysteriously alters and providence enters the situation to make it fruitful.

Our excursion into Narnia has only focused on one type of expectation, and there are many others. There is, for instance, the expectation of being used to the maximum of one's capacities from week two—at the latest—of one's arrival in the parish. The desire to be highly active at once, with little appreciation of the importance of being passive, especially in the first six months or so, is often the cause of considerable suffering. The difficulty is increased because the priestly ministry is primarily an active ministry, so that it is easy to make the mistake of thinking you are only fulfilling it when you are being active, and that you are being deprived of your rights if you are given less responsibility than you expect. But should that happen, it may be that God is giving you the opportunity to learn what it means to be passive, that is, to watch, to listen, to hold your peace, and, above all, to pray. Only so will the foundation be laid for an activity which will be truly effective.

But if you do find yourself complaining about your vicar's reluctance to delegate responsibility, let not the phrase, 'I think he/she finds me threatening' pass your lips! And should you even detect the thought in your heart, root it out with all possible speed! Growth in the Christian life is growth in self-knowledge, and to think of oneself as a threat to those placed over one is a device of the ego to prevent one from taking a hard look at oneself and so growing in self-knowledge. The use of that popular phrase is usually an indication that it is not so much a person's gifts which are found threatening but their faults with which the other person is unable to cope.

This inability on the part of the vicar to cope with the new deacon's failings is one of the difficulties the newly-ordained is likely to meet. A consequence is a sense of being left to live the Christian life at his or her own level without formation of an objective kind in the priestly vocation such as one receives in the religious life on going into a community. The problem is compounded because your theological college will, in all probability, have taken the view that you are going to learn all you need to know in the parish; and the parish will take the view that you have learnt all you need to know in your theological college. And so you may suffer from a sense of being left to sink or swim, for it too often happens that priests who have charge of deacons seem not to expect to train them in the way that, in our case, novice guardians expect to train those in their charge. However, the situation I am describing is much less likely to arise than it once was. There are good things happening behind the scenes in our Church, and one of them is the thought which is now being given to the care of deacons.

Nevertheless, even if you find yourself in an ideal situation, all expectations fully realised: a congenial and helpful vicar, surrounded by a group of the finest Christians you could hope to meet, set within a lively and caring parish, there is yet one source of suffering we should touch on, one which will not, I think, have formed any part of your expectations, and that is God.

Now in foreseeing God as a source of suffering we touch on your expectations concerning yourself. If they are fairly low God will probably leave you in peace—insofar as peace is possible in our human condition—because he is so gracious, and respects our free will so much, that he will not fight us unless we are prepared to fight with him against ourselves, that is, fight with him in rooting out all that hinders our spiritual growth. If this latter is the case we must be ready for trials which merely use the externals of our situation but are, in reality, due to what God is doing in our souls. For this reason we should be careful not to put the blame on any factor in our situation but recognise that whatever troubles us is being used by God for our ultimate good.

But more difficult to cope with, because more mysterious, is the unexpected way he deprives us of himself at the very moment when we thought to have more of him. The Song of Hezekiah (Isaiah 38:10–20) vividly conveys the feelings of a soul when, beginning to live the vocation to which it has so long been looking forward, and to which, after all, God himself has called it, he strikes it down and leaves it in a state of dereliction. But he does not leave it there for long because when the soul has suffered this mysterious interior death for a time it begins to see that, as the Song says, 'in all these things' it has suffered 'is the life of its spirit'. And although this text may be more applicable to the postulant during the first terrible months after entering a monastery, I have known deacons suffer similarly, so, in the best Puddleglum manner, I throw in the warning, that you may not be unduly dismayed if the like should happen to you.

> I said in the cutting off of my days, I shall go to the gates of the grave; I am deprived of the residue of my years.
>
> I said, I shall not see the Lord, even the Lord, in the land of the living; I shall behold man no more with the inhabitants of the world.
>
> Mine age is departed, and is removed from me as a shepherd's tent.
>
> I have cut off like a weaver my life; he will cut me off with pining sickness; from day even to night wilt thou make an end of me.
>
> I reckoned till morning, that, as a lion, so will he break my all bones; from day even to night wilt thou make an end of me.
>
> Like a crane or a swallow, so did I chatter; I did mourn as a dove.
>
> Mine eyes fail with looking upward; O Lord, I am oppressed; undertake for me.
>
> What shall I say? He hath both spoken to me, and himself hath done it. I shall go softly all my years in the bitterness of my soul.
>
> O Lord, by these things men live, and in all these things is the life of my spirit; so wilt thou recover me, and make me to live.

Behold, for peace I had great bitterness; but thou hast in love to my soul delivered it from the pit of corruption; for thou hast cast all my sins behind thy back.

For the grave cannot praise thee, death cannot celebrate thee; they that go down to the pit cannot hope for thy truth.

The living, the living, he shall praise thee, as I do this day; the father to the children shall make known thy truth.

The Lord was ready to save me; therefore we will sing my songs to the stringed instruments all the days of our life in the house of the Lord.

Isaiah 38:10–20

* * * * *

III

POVERTY

In the prelude to George Herbert's *A Priest to the Temple or The Country Parson*, he writes: 'I have resolved to set down the Form and Character of a true Pastor that I may have a mark to aim at: which also I will set as high as I can, since he shoots higher that threatens the Moon than he that aims at a Tree.'

Having discouraged you in our last talk from threatening your vicar, I hope you will bear with me in the next three while I threaten the moon by attempting to expound what are traditionally called the 'Evangelical Counsels' or 'Counsels of Perfection', namely, Poverty, Chastity and Obedience. These 'general counsels', as they are designated, have become associated with the Religious Life which has, in the course of the centuries, made them the subject of vows, with nullifying effect on their application to Christians whose vocation does not lie within the Religious Life. But it was not always so, and my intention is to show that they remain fundamental for whatever form the Christian vocation takes and can, in particular, be applied to the priestly vocation.

All these 'counsels' are open to serious misunderstanding and conflicting interpretation, our first one, Poverty, not least. The word poverty can be taken at many different levels of meaning and it is especially liable to misinterpretation when used in any sense other than the literal one. It is, indeed, something of a Humpty-Dumpty word which means whatever the Humpty-Dumpty propounding it intends it to mean. So one needs to be rather flexible about it for it means different things in different contexts. For instance, the phrase 'poverty of spirit' is sometimes employed to mean an impoverished soul, a state of unblessedness the very opposite of what is intended in the beatitude, 'Blessed are the poor in spirit'. Similarly, the state of poverty a few consciously undertake in the Religious Life is not to be confused, much less compared, with the poverty in which many are forced to live. In what follows we will be concerned with poverty of spirit in the sense of the beatitude, that is, with dispossession, detachment and renunciation. The Rule of the Sisters of the Love of God puts it thus:

> Monastic poverty is more than a simplification of life in a community of common ownership. It means an entire dependence on Christ, in whom all things are gathered and in whom all things are possessed. This is the holy indifference which is true liberty.

The key phrase in that passage is 'entire dependence on Christ'. Only in him and through him and for him may we possess what we do possess. But this entire dependence on Christ is made possible only by Christ himself who 'though he was in the form of God, did not count equality with God a thing to be grasped, but emptied himself, taking the form of a servant' (Phil. 2:6–7). It is Christ's self-emptying which opens the way for our self-emptying.

But there is a crucial difference between the self-emptying of Christ and our self-emptying. He emptied himself of what was truly his, of the glory that was his with the Father before the world began (John 17:5). Our self-emptying is of what is not truly ours, of those acquisitions of mind and feelings we have been accumulating since our own little world began and which stand between us and the glory God desires for us. The question is not whether our acquisitions are good or bad but the extent to which they are unconscious and automatic; whether they use us, or whether we are free enough in relation to them to make a right use of them. Such freedom, such true liberty, only comes from self-emptying, from our practice of poverty of spirit in the circumstances to which God has called each one of us.

Now the circumstances into which he will call you may, for some, include a ministry to people living in poverty at its most literal level. And for any thus called what will be important is the call, for it is the call which will give you the grace to work and worship in the midst of apparent hopelessness without becoming crushed and confused by it. But every one of you will be called at some time or another to face tragedy, injustice, inequality and human wretchedness of every kind. You will be called to care for those who are poor and needy in some form or other, for that is what your vocation demands of you.

> Is not this the fast that I choose:
> to loose the bonds of wickedness
> to undo the thongs of the yoke
> to let the oppressed go free
> and to break every yoke?
> Is it not to share your bread with the hungry
> and bring the homeless poor into your house;
> when you see the naked, to cover him
> and not to hide yourself from your own flesh?
>
> Isaiah 58:6 ff.

To loose the bonds of wickedness, to undo the thongs of the yoke, to let the oppressed go free, and to break every yoke, means to act in an infinite variety of ways according to circumstances. There is no misery which does not concern your ministry, and if you find yourself called into conflict with the temporal powers in your efforts to loose the bonds of wickedness, to free the oppressed, and to break every yoke, let not talk of political action being inappropriate to the priestly function deflect you. Christianity is not a department of life: it is the whole of life. So it is right that you should become identified with whatever sufferings or serious issues you may have to face, and to work for their recognition and alleviation. Nevertheless, it is precisely in becoming identified with a cause that one may betray it. So we need to be clear about this word 'identification'.

There are two ways of becoming identified: the first way occurs when, for whatever reason, the ego is aroused and attaches itself to a particular cause, let us say, to racism. It will then be the ego, now identified with this cause, which works on its behalf. Such identification is the antithesis of poverty of spirit, and these are the signs: it is elated by success, cast down by failure, enraged by criticism, sustained by self-righteousness. It engages in acrimonious controversy, does not restrain itself from scoring debating points, even in matters of life and death, and seizes not only its adversaries but also its sympathisers by the throat—down which it thrusts its message. Finally, at the end of a very hard day, it retires into its corner sobbing with self-pity. Kierkegaard, in a chapter called 'The Egocentric Service of the Good', says something similar:

Alas, men often enough confuse impatience with humble, obedient enthusiasm; impatience even lends itself to this confusion. When a man is active early and late 'for the sake of the Good,' storming about noisily and restlessly, hurling himself into time, as a sick man throws himself down upon his bed, throwing off all consideration for himself, as a sick man throws off his clothes, scornful of the world's reward; when such a man makes a place among men, then the masses think what he himself imagines, that he is inspired... He cannot, he will not, understand the Good's slowness; that out of mercy the Good is slow; that out of love for free persons, it will not use force; that in its wisdom toward the frail ones, it shrinks from any deception. He cannot, he will not, humbly understand that the Good can get on without him. He is double-minded, he that with his enthusiasm could apparently become an apostle, but can quite as readily become a Judas, who treacherously wishes to hasten the victory of the Good. He is scandalised, he that by his enthusiasm seems to love the Good so highly. He is scandalised by its poverty, when it is clothed in the slowness of time. He is not devoted to the Good in service that may profit nothing. He only effervesces, and he that effervesces loves the moment.[7]

The second way of becoming identified is the way of love, the way of the one who emptied himself, taking the form of a servant. And of this way Kierkegaard writes:

> The Good puts on the slowness of time as a poor garment, and in keeping with this change of dress one who serves it must be clothed in the insignificant figure of the unprofitable servant. With the eye of his senses he is not permitted to see the Good in victory. Only with the eye of faith can he strive after its eternal victory.[8]

In contrast to the double-minded person who 'is not content with the blessed assurance which comforts beyond all measure,' the one who serves knows

> that eternally the Good has always been victorious; the blessed assurance which is a security that passeth all understanding; the blessed assurance that the unprofitable servant may have within himself at each moment, even when the time is longest and he seems to have accomplished least of all, the blessed assurance which allows the unprofitable servant if he loses honour to speak more proudly than that royal word: All is lost save honour. And when even honour is lost to say: Nothing is lost, but all is gained.[9]

Yes, to lose all, even honour, and yet to consider that all is gained, is the way of poverty of spirit. But such poverty of spirit is rare. It is the narrow gate which in the gospel of Matthew we are invited to enter by Jesus:

> Enter by the narrow gate; for wide is the gate and easy the way that leads to destruction, and many are they who go therein. For narrow is the gate and hard the way that leads to life, and few there are who find it.   7:13–14

---

[7] From *Purity of Heart*, Harper Torchbooks, New York, 1956, pp. 101–102.
[8] Ibid., p. 103.
[9] Ibid., p. 102.

But if we should stumble on it, because grace has been our guide, how amazing are those rewards for which we never dared to look.

> Assuredly, I say to you, there is no one who has left house or brothers or sisters or father or mother or wife or children or lands for my sake and the gospel's, who shall not receive a hundredfold now in this time—houses and brothers and sisters and mothers and children and lands, with persecutions, and in the age to come eternal life.
>
> Mark 10:29–30

That text is invariably used in connection with the Religious Life, and understood according to the literal sense it is clearly more applicable to Religious than to those following other paths. Certainly the history of countless religious foundations bears out the truth of the passage taken literally, for examine the beginnings of the greatest monastic houses and you will find that their origins were obscure, humble and poor. The greater the renunciation, the greater the abandonment to divine providence in founding a community, the greater the riches of all kinds which subsequently pour in. But Jesus' words are not addressed to monks; they are addressed to disciples—and to be a disciple is open to all of us. And to all he propounds a spiritual law in this text: Give up your relationships and your territories at the level of possessions and they will be returned to you a hundredfold as gifts. It is an interior disposition he requires, and we have to learn to experience the taste of it for ourselves and recognise when we are clinging on to our responsibilities and family obligations in a way which hinders their being constantly renewed in Christ. Here is Kierkegaard again:

> One man says, 'I am not justified in doing that because of my wife and children'... But I wonder if he, as man and father, really could do anything better for wife and children than to impress upon them this trust in Providence. Here, then, it is not as in civil life that the person who risks dares hope that the

state will look after his wife and children. No, spiritually understood, he has by his venture cared for them in the best possible way, for by this he has shown them that he at least has faith in Providence.[10]

Now this faith in providence, on which the spirit of poverty rests, is, among many other marvels, the surest safeguard against certain kinds of fruitless, time-consuming misfortunes which so easily befall people in whom there is no such trust. Therefore to develop in oneself this trust is a great thing for by it we help the truly poor—that is, those who do not know that Christ came to make them rich—more than in any other way.

But if it is a great thing to develop it is not an easy thing. Moreover, it is easily lost, and so God tests us in it from time to time. If, then, I draw back on the grounds that to respond to this demand will involve me in endless such demands so that at this rate I will soon be ruined or brought to the edge of a breakdown, or the balance of my vocation will be unduly upset, then far from saving what I possess I will be imperceptibly impoverished. The spirit of poverty, lived in total reliance on the Holy Spirit, does not involve us in repetitious and ruinous demands. It involves us in demands—yes! But they are always different, and they are always ultimately enriching, never impoverishing.

To know the truth of this, however, we have to learn what it means to cast our bread upon the waters—as the author of Ecclesiastes directs us to do (11:1). And that never becomes any easier. There is always a painful moment of choice, as fresh and as difficult as though one had never cast one's bread on the waters before, and never known the amazing returns one has had. It always feels as though this time one really is being asked too much! And yet, if one responds, not because of the sake of any return but because of a suspicion

---

[10] From the chapter, 'The Price of Willing One Thing', op. cit. p. 130.

that behind that all too human being who is making the demand our heavenly Father is waiting for our 'yes', then the law of increasing returns comes into operation and we find ourselves the gainers by thirty, sixty, a hundred fold.

For you know the grace of our Lord Jesus Christ, that though he was rich, yet for your sake he became poor, so that by his poverty you might become rich.

II Cor. 8:9

In the world as it is, with all its inequalities, maldistribution of goods, starvation and misery of every kind, of which we are ceaselessly made aware through the media, the fact of our becoming rich in Christ is one about which many Christians, especially Religious, rightly agonise. We are embarrassed because we are not suffering similarly. But I think we are embarrassed about the wrong thing. For if we are living in a spirit of renunciation we should not be embarrassed to find that Christ's promises are fulfilled: 'I came that you might have life, and have it more abundantly' (John 10:10). It is, as we have seen, a spiritual law which is open to everyone, and what we should be embarrassed about is that we fail to teach it. We fail the amazing promises of the Gospel by worrying about whether we should be literally poor instead of revealing to the poor what is necessary to become rich.

The difficulty is, as we acknowledge with sorrow, that not all of us are capable of the radical renunciation, the utter dispossession of self, the wholehearted trust in God and in his human agents, which are necessary if he is to find a space in us large enough to pour in his treasures so that they overflow into a world desperately in need of them. Perhaps it is that the spirit of poverty is itself a gift, and that we are only given it if we earnestly desire it.

But let us suppose we have received this gift—in however small a degree. What can then happen, when its inevitable corollary flows in, is that we even seem to have become too rich; we seem to have been given almost more than we can

23

cope with. And perhaps that is what the curious addition, 'with persecutions', in our text from Mark might mean. For 'Unto whomsoever much is given, of the same shall much be required' (Luke 12:48), and the ministers in a parish, and their spouses, or the members of a religious community, can at times suffer a sense of intangible persecution when much is being given which entails much being required of them. But if this 'much' does indeed become 'too much' it is because we are not being faithful to our times of self-emptying, namely, our times of prayer. It is these times which restore the balance, regulate our lives, check demands beyond our capacity, and renew our dependence on him who knows what we need and of what we are capable.

Nevertheless, in regard to actual material possessions the sense of having too much should always be with us. It is good to delight in beauty, and to make our homes a joy to live in, but treasures turn to trash, spiritually speaking, if the spirit of acquisitiveness is not constantly being curbed. A passage quoted in *Christian Asceticism and Modern Man* puts it well: 'He who has the spirit of poverty always has too much and tends always to be cutting down... He who has the spirit of the world never has enough, is never content, and always wants something more.'[11]

All this leads us to a very important text, recorded in Mark and Luke and twice in Matthew: 'For to him who has will more be given, and he will have abundance; but from him who has not, even what he has will be taken away' (Matt. 13:12; 25:29, Mark 4:25, Luke 8:18). In the terms of our theme we may say that to everyone who has the spirit of poverty, that is, the spirit which is always willing to empty itself for another and to say: 'yes, I have time for you; yes, I have what you want, please take it; yes, I have more than I need, please share in my abundance', then to that spirit more will always

---

[11] Blackfriars Publications, London, 1955, p. 234.

be given. But the spirit which says: 'no, I have no time; no, I have not got what you want, and would be unwilling to give it to you if I had; no, I have so little that I cannot possibly share it', then from that spirit will be taken away what little it has, for every time we close the door of our response we put ourselves under the law of diminishing returns. Most of us are one thing one day and another the next. What is important is to recognise the spirit in which we are acting, never to justify ourselves, and daily to stretch our spiritual muscles in the direction of positive response; if, that is, we want our lives to become ever richer, more interesting, and radiant with the spirit of Christ.

Finally, on the counsel of Poverty, our self-emptying, as we have seen, is dependent on Christ's self-emptying, and just as his self-emptying brought him before Pilate, to be mocked and scourged and crucified, so our self-emptying, if it is to be real, must be complemented by the emptying which others inflict on us, the hurts, the humiliations, the criticisms, insults even, and everything which we now label 'diminishment of the person'. Oh blessed diminishment! Where would our growth in holiness be without it!

This is where, I believe, the Religious Life has the edge on any other for it has always understood the importance of humiliations (though at times in its history it has gravely misapplied that understanding), and therefore teaches those called to it how to accept them in a spirit which will make them fruitful. For us, constantly to be brought down in lowliness is what being in community is all about, and although we don't like it any better than anyone else, and are even, it has to be admitted, pretty soft about it these days, we all know that our growth in the spirit, in the hope of which we entered the community, depends upon it. But for lyrical praise of this fruitful soil I turn not to a writer from the monastic tradition but to a Baptist minister, John Bunyan, who knew well of what he wrote:

Then said Mr Great-Heart, 'We need not be so afraid of this Valley of Humiliation, for here is nothing to hurt us, unless we procure it to ourselves... Behold, how green this valley is; also how beautiful with lilies. I have known many labouring men that have got good estates in this Valley of Humiliation; for God resisteth the proud, but gives more, more grace to the humble. For indeed, it is a very fruitful soil, and doth bring forth by handfuls. Some also have wished that the next way to their Father's house were here, that they might be troubled no more with either hills or mountains to go over, but the way is the way, and there's an end...

Then said Mercy, 'I think I am as well in this Valley as I have been anywhere else... Methinks, here one may, without much molestation, be thinking what he is, whence he came, what he has done, and to what the King has called him. Here one may think, and break at heart, and melt in one's spirit, until one's eyes become as the fish-pools of Heshbon. They that go rightly through this Valley of Bacha, make it a well; the rain that God sends down from heaven upon them that are here, also filleth the pools. This Valley is that from whence also the King will give to their vineyards, and they that go through it shall sing...

The Pilgrim's Progress, Part the Second

* * * * *

IV

CHASTITY

Our second 'counsel of perfection' is chastity, and because of the dedication of our Community to the Love of God we regard it as the one most central to our ethos. Not that it is possible to separate the Evangelical Counsels, for 'in this trinity none is afore, or after other: none is greater or less than another'—to borrow from the Athanasian Creed. But for us there is an emphasis on the 'dignity and power of holy chastity', as the SLG Rule expresses it, which ineluctably follows from the Community's distinctive dedication to the mystery of the love of God.

Chastity is generally confused with celibacy, and certainly in the case of religious the vow of Chastity is understood to include perpetual celibacy, an understanding which is stated explicitly in our Rule. But this assimilation of chastity to celibacy has resulted in a widespread misunderstanding of the term. For chastity is not promoted by celibacy, neither is it hindered by marriage. Chastity is attained by loving: by loving a person, by loving wisdom, by loving God. But if you ask: what then is the point of celibacy? I would reply that it is to do with the New Dispensation, with the indwelling of Christ, and with the call to some Christians to respond to that indwelling by celibacy—which is not to be taken to mean that Christ does not indwell all the baptised equally. I refer only to a particular response.

But celibacy is not our subject. What I shall talk about is chastity: chastity of soul, purity of heart, singleness of will, the spirit of love, and what it is in our created nature—especially as we have come to understand it over the last hundred or so years—which hinders these virtues. But first of all, let us begin with some passages from William Law's *The*

27

Spirit of Love, which is permeated by the idea of God dwelling in the soul.

> Would you know the blessing of all blessings? It is this God of love dwelling in your soul and killing every root of bitterness which is the pain and torment of every earthly, selfish love. For all wants are satisfied, all disorders of nature are removed, no life is any longer a burden, every day is a day of peace, everything you meet becomes a help to you, because everything you see or do is all done in the sweet, gentle element of love. For as love has no by-ends, wills nothing but its own increase, so everything is as oil to its flame. It must have that which it wills and cannot be disappointed, because everything naturally helps it to live in its own way and to bring forth its own work. The spirit of love does not want to be rewarded, honoured, or esteemed. Its only desire is to propagate itself and become the blessing and happiness of everything that wants it. And therefore it meets wrath and evil and hatred and opposition with the same one will as the light meets the darkness, only to overcome it with all its blessings...[12]

Then Law goes on to discuss what he calls 'the first created nature' of the soul:

> There is no peace, nor ever can be, for the soul of man but in the purity and perfection of its first created nature; nor can it have its purity and perfection in any other way than in and by the spirit of love. For as love is the God that created all things, so love is the purity, the perfection, and blessing of all created things; and nothing can live in God but as it lives in love. Look at every vice, pain, and disorder in human nature; it is in itself nothing else but the spirit of the creature turned from the universality of love to some self-seeking or own will in created things...
>
> Purification therefore is the one thing necessary, and nothing will do in the stead of it. But man is not purified till every earthly, wrathful, sensual, selfish, partial self-willing temper is taken from him. He is not dying to himself till he is dying to

---

[12] *Works*, Vol. VIII, London, 1893 reprint of the 1762 edition.

these tempers, and he is not alive in God till he is dead to them.[13]

'There is no peace', he says, 'nor ever can be for the soul but in the purity of its first created nature.' And because we have lost the purity of our first created nature, purification becomes 'the one thing necessary'.

But what is our first created nature except in the purity of which there is no peace? If we look carefully into the matter we find we have two created natures.

And God said, Let us make man in our image, after our likeness... So God created man in his own image, in the image of
God created he him: male and female created he them.

Gen. 1:26,27

Our 'first created nature' comes from our being made in the image and likeness of God, a text which has provided the Church with a key, much used by the early Fathers, with which to understand the nature of our created humanity in relation to God our Creator. It is, moreover, like many keys from the Old Testament, one which could only be turned when the Incarnation of our Lord and Saviour Jesus Christ, revealed to the world both perfect image and perfect likeness; when the breach between image and likeness, caused by sin, had been repaired by the perfect life of God made man. According to this doctrine, the image of God in the soul is in-destructible while the likeness to God can only be restored by work, by turning from 'unlikeness' to his likeness and so to our true selves, as St Bernard wrote in a sermon called 'On recovering the likeness through love.'[14]

The second account of the creation of human beings has a remarkably different feel about it, one which bears a striking resemblance to the evolutionary theories, with their descrip-tion of sentient beings emerging gradually from the

---

[13] Ibid.
[14] From his *Sermons on the Song of Songs*, No. 83.

primordial slime:

> Then went up a mist from the earth, and watered the whole
> face of the ground. And the Lord God formed man of the dust
> of the ground, and breathed into his nostrils the breath of life;
> and man became a living soul. Gen. 2:6–7

For the early Church Father, Origen, the two accounts
reveal the making of two men: the first in the image and likeness of God, and the second formed of the slime of the earth.
The first is the inner man, destined for eternal life, and the
second is the outer man, subject to corruption. 'For if', says
Origen, quoting St Paul (II Cor. 4:16), 'our outward man is
corrupted yet the inward man is renewed day by day.'[15]
Modern biblical commentators explain the two accounts differently, but in a way which fits with Origen, the first
account, they say, being a doctrinal one (the Priestly), concerned wholly with God and what he is doing, while the
second account (the Yahwist) is a narrative in which the
primary theme is centred on man and the earth. 'It is man's
world', Gerhard von Rad writes of this second account, 'the
world of his life...which God, in what follows, establishes
around man.'[16]

If we look at the last two thousand years in the light of the
Incarnation, and with the belief that it is the Word made flesh
who provides the key to the mysteries of the Old Testament,
we might say that the first account of creation belongs to the
first millennium AD, and was worked out in the mystical
theology of the Fathers and the doctrinal grapplings of the
great Ecumenical Councils. The second account, the world of
man, seems to belong equally well to the second millennium,
and has been fully plumbed in this last part of it, notably by
followers of Darwin, Freud and Marx, the way for them

---

[15] *Commentary on the Song of Songs*, trans. R. P. Lawson in Ancient Christian
Writers, London, 1957, p. 25.
[16] *Genesis*, London, ET 1961, p. 74. Author's italics.

having been paved by the philosophy of the Enlightenment, especially in Germany, in combining 'opposition to all supernatural religion and belief in the all-sufficiency of human reason with an ardent desire to promote the happiness of men in this life.'[17] If, then, we agree to regard Christ as the key which unlocked the developments suggested by the two accounts of creation, we may say that the first millennium AD was concerned with divinity and the second with humanity —which, indeed, they have been, whatever the explanation.

But humanity, in plumbing its own depths, has lost, through its acceptance of the theory of evolution, its sense of divine provenance. In the light of the interpretation of the last 2,000 years I have suggested, this clearly is part of the divine plan. But it has consequences which I am not sure Christians have yet fully faced—probably because Christendom has been anxious to forget the foolish impression its spokesmen made on popular opinion by their initial reactions to *The Origin of Species* (1859) and *The Descent of Man* (1871). It is an ironical thought that if these books had appeared in Origen's day the course of the debate between scientists and Christians would have run differently, for since Origen did not interpret the Bible literally he would not have been concerned about the threat to its literal understanding. But he would certainly have been concerned about the threat to the spiritual understanding of the scriptures.

What the theory of evolution might mean at the spiritual level if properly understood is not at all clear—though we have been given marvellous rays of light on the question by Teilhard de Chardin. What is clear is that its application to both Old and New Testaments has almost imperceptibly done much to diminish their influence on our lives. For evolution implies progress, and progress implies that we

---

[17] From the article 'Aufklärung' (Germ., 'Enlightenment'), *Oxford Dictionary of the Christian Church*, 1974.

know better. And if we know better than the biblical writers, what does that do to their influence on us?

So the evolutionary theory poses problems for faith. And it is on faith that morals depend. Nevertheless, in 1984, to mark the 100th anniversary of Darwin's death, the Pontifical Academy of Sciences accepted a working draft which states: 'We are convinced that masses of evidence render the application of the concept of evolution to man and the other primates beyond serious dispute.' The report went on: 'The evolutionary development of life, specifically including that of the physical body of man, was finally pronounced acceptable by the Holy See as a working scientific hypothesis which, properly understood, constitutes no danger to faith and morals.'[18]

'Properly understood'—yes, that is the crux of the matter. Certainly, in the careful words, 'a working scientific hypothesis', much has been understood, for the 'masses of evidence' have not yet amounted to proof even if they 'render the concept of evolution...beyond serious dispute'. But it is surely rash to pronounce the evolutionary theory one which constitutes no danger to faith and morals. How is the shift from the belief that man is made in the divine image to the belief that he is the apex of the evolutionary process to be understood in a way which does not radically alter faith and morals? Is it not a stupendous shift? And are not the consequences of it already evident in every sphere of life? Inventiveness run riot, genetic engineering, the domination of the media, pollution, noise, rush, restlessness and the ceaseless chatter of our society? All this is, I believe, too coincidental with the assumption of an anthropoid ancestry to be other than the result of it.

In an address called 'Recollection' the late Gilbert Shaw said: 'The essential characteristic of our being in the image of

---

[18] *The Tablet*, 4 February 1984, p. 102.

God is freedom... But we are always striving in some way to divest ourselves of our freedom and to sink into some kind of merely natural order, into some kind of temporal conditioning or ideology which saves us having to face ourselves and our neighbour in the light of God.' [19] That well describes, I think, the spirit in which the Western world has swallowed the evolutionary theory, and since 'We are what we eat', in Feuerbach's notable dictum, we are increasingly manifesting an anthropoidal character, living more and more according to our 'second created nature', to our outer man, the one subject to corruption.

It is this which imperils our world and which as Christians we must strive, by God's grace, to counter. And I think we do this by facing the similarities we recognise in ourselves with the anthropoids so that we may strive, on the contrary, to attain to that freedom which belongs to our being made in the image of God. For 'there is no peace', you will recall, 'nor ever can be for the soul of man but in the purity and perfection of its first created nature.'

Now in what ways do we manifest similarities with our anthropoid ancestors? Their characteristics are well known and, avoiding those which are not seemly to mention, we can take three for our purpose. First, they never stop chattering, second, they never stop twitching, and third, they always crowd together. In apes these characteristics are proper to their nature; in humans they hinder spiritual growth and, in particular, they hinder the development not only of the dignity of chastity but of its power. Therefore we must learn to be silent, learn to be still, and learn what it means to resist the lure of the multitude. Let us look at these requirements.

First of all, we will accomplish all three at once if, above all, we remain faithful to our Office. For the words we sing or speak in the Office belong to our silence; the movements nec-

---

[19] For Trinity XXIII, 1966. Gilbert Shaw was our Warden at the time.

essary for performing the Office belong to our stillness; and the people with whom we may perform the Office belong to our solitude.

Secondly, we will again accomplish all three in our times of silent prayer (which, in a properly organised and disciplined life, should amount to not less than one half-hour a day). It is in these times that we will become most painfully aware of the ape within, expressed not physically but in our circling thoughts. Our thoughts do, indeed, go round and round most of the time, and some situations provoke endless repetitions, not only of the same thoughts but of the same words so that our minds are like old gramophone records, stuck in a groove, tirelessly repeating themselves—the mental equivalent of what in monkeys is their way of never leaving themselves alone. This—the subject is immaterial—is unchastity in its most deep-rooted and subtle form, the breeding-ground of a lack of purity, of one-pointedness, of power in life itself. And although our times of silent prayer will seldom be free of circling thoughts, it is here, by the grace of God—and his grace only—that the needle is lifted and something new and fresh, we know not what, comes in to give freedom to the soul.

But even if our half-hour has passed without much sense of the needle having been lifted, we need not be discouraged, for at such times the thoughts which hold us in their grip are coming up for purification—that purification which is 'the one thing necessary'. Moreover, behind all the monkey chatter, the soul, unperceived by the conscious mind, is rapt in the love of God. We know this by an obscure sense that however badly the time may seem to have gone we would not wish to have been deprived of it. And we would not be deprived of it, not only for what it mysteriously brings us at the time, but because all else hangs on it—and for the priest what hangs on it is the depth and purity, the silence and stillness, with which he or she celebrates the Eucharist.

34

And thirdly, in our home and in our pastoral work, we need to cultivate the spirit of silence, stillness and solitude, everything, that is, which is meant by the word 'recollection'. Recollection is mysteriously dependent on grace, but our part is to practise it here and there, dropping what we are doing for a few moments, sitting still and letting go of our tensions, allowing our thoughts to fall away and replacing them with a brief glimpse of the silence and stillness of Jesus in his humanity. The ape in us is profoundly reluctant to do this, indeed, incapable of doing it, so it is a real struggle against nature. But if we are resolved upon it, we will be aided by God's grace, and then we will find that our life becomes more measured, and that our contacts with people move more in the direction of the Communion of Saints rather than back into the hectic fellowship of the monkey-house.

* * *

In the story of the 'Woman taken in adultery' (John 8:1–11), we see the chastity of Jesus manifested in all its perfection. In the first place, he remains silent when the scribes and Pharisees challenge him on the law of Moses in the hope of finding something to use against him. He remains silent, I think, because a life is at stake. On other occasions, when the questions put to him were hypothetical, he answered readily. But now he is silent. And by his silence the accusers are enabled to accuse themselves when they are faced with his question, 'If there is one among you who is without sin, let him be the first to cast a stone at her.' Jesus does not watch them as they slink away one by one for he is not standing in judgement on them any more than he now stands in judgement on the woman. And such a man can say not only, 'Neither do I condemn thee', but 'Go, and sin no more.'

The moral prescriptions of the New Testament, no less than those of the Old, are intended for a people who believe themselves to be made in the divine image, that is to say, they are not directed at the belief, now firmly established in the collective unconscious, that we are the result of an evolutionary process, with its nullifying effects on the notion of sin. Christians, therefore, are caught in a dilemma between the clear teaching of the New Testament on the one hand and its apparent inappropriateness in the present psychological climate on the other—a dilemma which affects us more disastrously than non-biblical religions because we have a foot in both beliefs and are consequently torn apart when moral conflict arises.

Your ministry over the years will be fraught with moral and ethical problems, which is the reason for your overwhelming need of chastity. But not for you is the pseudo-chastity of former times which stood cold and aloof on the bank delivering an improving sermon to the sinner sinking into the mire; nor the unchastity of the present times which, overcome with empathy, leaps in to be 'alongside'—until both disappear from sight. No, what you will need is a chastity which can kneel on the bank and hold on until, by the mercy of God, the other finds his own foothold, and can then be pulled out.

We have compassion because Jesus was always compassionate. Moreover, he told us that with what judgement we judge we shall be judged, and that with what measure we mete it shall be measured to us (Matt. 7:2). But it is questionable whether we can appropriate to ourselves the right to say, 'Neither do I condemn thee,' unless we also have the power to say, 'Sin no more'. And the power to say, 'Sin no more,' belongs only to perfect chastity. 'Therefore, my soul, be chaste.'

That last phrase is from Teilhard de Chardin, and I will end our counsel on Chastity with the passage from which it comes, not only for what it says but much more because Teilhard stands for a positive understanding of evolution, while he is, at the same time, a supreme example of a passionate chastity—a quite new phenomenon in Christian sanctity, and one that he himself saw would be essential for the survival of the human race.

Fold your wings, my soul, those wings you had spread wide to soar to the terrestrial peaks where the light is most ardent: it is for you simply to await the descent of the Fire—supposing it to be willing to take possession of you.

If you would attract its power to yourself you must first loosen the bonds of affection which still tie you to objects cherished too exclusively for their own sake. The true union you ought to seek with creatures that attract you is to be found not by going directly to them but by converging with them on God sought in and through them. It is not by making themselves more material, relying solely on physical contacts, but by making themselves more spiritual in the embrace of God that things draw closer to each other and, following their invincible natural bent, end by becoming, all of them together, one. Therefore, my soul, be chaste.[20]

* * * * *

[20] Pensée 36 from *Hymn of the Universe*, London, 1965, pp. 110–111.

V

OBEDIENCE

We believe in one God...maker...of all that is, seen and unseen.

In this talk I shall look at obedience in two parts; first, obedience to what is seen, and secondly, obedience to what is unseen. They are not, of course, to be divided, for what is seen is penetrated and sustained by what is unseen, while what is unseen can only be understood, this side of death, from the standpoint of the seen. Nevertheless, if I say that the talk will be first about obedience to human beings and secondly about obedience to angelic beings, that will give you some idea of what you are in for.

But before we can think about obedience at all we must take a look at what we think about God, for obedience is the fruit of our relationship with him; and it is only possible to the extent that we trust him. That is to say, the more we trust him, the more we believe in his omnipotence, the more we believe that not a sparrow falls to the ground except in the eternal purposes of an all-loving and all-powerful God, then the more shall we be able to be obedient to the people and circumstances of our life, for we will believe they are all playing a part in his eternal purposes for us.

If, on the other hand, our trust in God is still rather weak, if we cannot believe in him as all-powerful and all-caring at all times; if, indeed, in our heart of hearts we incline to think that beyond a certain point he is powerless to prevent things getting out of hand, or even if, not going so far, we rationalise God's failure to intervene as we think he should according to that popular doctrine of the 'Permissive Will', then we in our turn will be powerless to obey him beyond a certain point. And if we cannot obey him we will be unable to do those things which would lead to the fulfilment of our deepest desires, the fulfilment of all that he wishes for us in this life, and union in bliss with him in life eternal.

Now a lack of trust in God is, as we all know, the primal sin, the sin which cast Lucifer from heaven when, in his pride, it seemed to him that God was failing to run the universe quite as he, Lucifer, would have done it himself had a better providence put him in the place of God. And so, exiled from the bliss of union, he comes to abide in the torment of disunity. And wherever we find the spirit of criticism— 'murmuring,' as it is called in monastic writings—there he is.

And he is so pleasant, so plausible. 'Did God say...?' he begins in a tone of friendly enquiry, and instead of our replying, 'Yes, he did!' and promptly showing him the door, we become involved in explanations—and explanations suit his purpose admirably. Explanations reveal uncertainty, and uncertainty is based in lack of trust, and lack of trust is rooted in pride, and from pride springs disobedience. And when this train of cause and effect is set in motion one begins to see things with a beguiling clarity: 'the woman saw that the tree was good for food, and that it was a delight to the eyes...' (Gen. 3:6). Then the act of disobedience is committed, and the first consequence is that 'the eyes of both were opened.' 'The eyes that were then opened', says Origen, 'were their senses, which they had been keeping shut, and rightly so, for fear they should be distracted and so prevented from seeing with their spiritual eyes.'[21] And because the eyes of their senses were opened they at once saw what they had not seen before—that they were naked. And not only did they see themselves in this different way but they understood God differently for, as Adam confesses when God calls, 'Where are you?', he has become afraid of him, and so Adam hides himself because, as he says, he is naked. Their disobedience has radically altered their relationship with God for they now

---

[21] *Contra Celsum*, 7.39.

see things with eyes which make them hide from him; and, in hiding from him, he becomes hidden to them.

Thus the sin of disobedience condemned us to a vision which, however clear at the level of the senses, is blind in relation to that of the spirit. Thereafter this blindness belongs to our fallen state and will only be healed in 'that day' when, Isaiah tells us in his messianic prophecies, 'the eyes of the blind shall be opened' (Is. 29:18 and 35:5). And 'that day' has come. The obedience unto death of our Lord and Saviour Jesus Christ has effected the reversal of Adam's sin and given us the possibility of seeing again with our spiritual eyes. But this capacity does not belong to our fallen nature. We have, as it were, to claim it by the way we live, for it will not be granted to us to enjoy the fruits of our Redeemer's obedience if we ourselves fail in this very thing.

Now, so far are some of us in the Church from possessing the grace of obedience that, on the contrary, the spirit of democracy entering where it should not, we rather pride ourselves on our disobedience. In extenuation it is said that the problem of obedience is the problem of authority, and that where authority is weak, as it is in the Church of England— so the argument runs—then it is unrealistic to expect selfless obedience of its members. But would it not be unworthy of us, a betrayal of our moral courage, to obey authority because it had the appearance of strength?

A Benedictine abbot of the last century, Dom Columba Marmion, although breathing the spirit of an age altogether gone, had, I think, some timeless things to say on this question in his book, *Christ the Ideal of the Monk*, and if you substitute 'principal' or 'vicar' or 'bishop' for 'abbot' in the following passage you will, I hope, find it relevant:

> Men of the world sometimes reproach us religious for being characterless, servile or small-minded in face of authority...
> There is, in fact, something debasing for a man to obey another man, when the latter appears merely as a man, and not as

representing, in some degree, divine authority. To obey the Abbot because we have the same ideas or the same tastes as he has, because we feel for him a natural sympathy, because he possesses talents that we admire, because we find his orders are reasonable, is unworthy of us and apart from the virtue of obedience...

None of these natural motives ought ever to affect us. Why so? Because as soon as we place ourselves on the natural plane, one man is worth as much as another, and the dignity of man commands him not to submit to another creature, considered as such; to do so would be to lessen and abase himself. Never would I obey a man, were this man a dazzling genius, if he had not received a participation in the Divine authority in order to command me. But as soon as God says: 'Such or such a man represents Me', were this man without talents, had he all the most crying defects...I would yield myself to him—as long as he ordered me nothing contrary to the Divine law..."[22]

Let us now hear what Christ himself, the ideal of all Christians, has to say on this subject according to Matthew:

The scribes and the Pharisees sit in Moses' seat. All therefore whatsoever they bid you observe, that observe and do; but do not after their works; for they say, and do not.   23:1–3

Then Jesus goes on to describe these men he has just told us to obey. And if we substitute 'church leaders' for 'scribes and Pharisees' it will be clearer to us that what Jesus is talking about is the effect of religion on those who are temperamentally authoritarian:

All their works they do to be seen of men; they make broad their phylacteries and enlarge the borders of their garments, and love the uppermost rooms at feasts, and the chief seats in the synagogues, and greetings in the market place, and to be called, rabbi, rabbi...   23:5–7

At this point Jesus describes the kind of authority he demands of his disciples and concludes: 'He that is greatest

---

[22] Maredsous, 1922. Eng. trans. London, 1926, pp. 272–3.

among you shall be your servant. And whosoever shall exalt himself shall be abased; and he that shall humble himself shall be exalted.' And then he returns to his indictment of the wrong exercise of authority with the 'seven woes' passage which begins (in my version): 'Woe unto you, bishops and patriarchs, hypocrites! for ye shut up the kingdom of heaven against men', and ends: 'Woe unto you, priests and presbyters, hypocrites! for ye are like unto whited sepulchres, which indeed appear beautiful outwardly, but are full of dead men's bones and of all uncleanness. Even so, ye also outwardly appear righteous unto men, but within ye are full of hypocrisy and iniquity' (Matt. 23:27–28).

This is hardly the tone of a man who is hoping for a seat in the House of Lords! Rather, it is the tone of a man who fears no one, who is free in relation to authority, of a man, that is, who seeks nothing for himself and therefore neither submits out of servitude nor reacts from self-will. Such a man has authority. And such a man said: 'The church leaders sit in the seats of authority. All therefore whatsoever they bid you observe, that observe and do.'

What happens then, you might ask? To see what happens when our Lord's injunctions are fully obeyed we have to look in the lives of the saints, and for our encouragement in this difficult matter we will look briefly at three saints whose lives exemplify the virtue of obedience when it is understood and practised to a supernatural degree.

The first is Ignatius of Loyola. After founding the Society of Jesus, Ignatius went to Rome where he was in close contact with the Pope and the papal court. What he saw led him to add a fourth vow to the traditional three: implicit obedience to the Pope himself. I do not know if the effect on the papacy of this vow was ever noticed but certainly, on looking at it from the side of the Popes, the curious fact emerges that the papacy has never, in the common phrase, been the same since. Paul III was the Pope who received this vow, and his

Renaissance magnificence, his mistress, his children, and his apparently irredeemable worldliness, must have appalled the austere convert to the cross. And yet Ignatius bowed his head and quite gratuitously undertook to obey. From then on Paul's own life began to change and he became increasingly concerned with reform, while since his time subsequent Popes have always been Popes, that is, marked by a distinctively religious character and not, as by Paul III's time they had become, the most sumptuous potentates in Christendom.

Secondly, there is the example of Pope John XXIII, whose obedience was of a similar kind to that of Ignatius, by whose Spiritual Exercises he was profoundly influenced. The fame of Pope John will always rest on his calling of the Second Vatican Council by which he set in motion a major revolution in the history of the Church. But it is salutary to remember that God did not use a revolutionary to carry out his revolution. Pope John's biographers sometimes fail to understand the significance of his obedient spirit as when, for instance, Meriol Trevor calls his reaction to Modernism 'conventional and naive,' after quoting from his diary: 'Jesus...has deigned to give me an even clearer understanding of the necessity of keeping whole and intact my "sense of faith" and my "being of one mind" with the Church... The worst of it is that ideas lead very swiftly to a spirit of independence and private judgement about everything and everyone.'[23] He may, at one level, have been wrong, but it was because he was granted this understanding, and obeyed it to a heroic degree in the face of very great personal suffering, that he succeeded to a position where his being 'of one mind' with the Church enabled him to change the mind of the Church. He was, indeed, an outstanding example of the truth of the Zen saying: 'You cannot change anything until you have accepted everything.'

---

[23] *Pope John*, London, 1967, p. 89.

My third example, Teresa of Avila, likewise possessed a profound understanding of the Church and of her place in it. 'I am a daughter of the Church' were almost her last words, and it was the love she had for the Church which was the motive of her obedience. But it also sprang from that self-mistrust of those who know their own power, who have experienced their ability to influence people and situations, and who are therefore fearful of failing, through self-will, to be a channel of the Divine will. Disobedience, on the contrary, Teresa saw to be based on a failure of the will to become united with the Divine will. And such a will compensates for its impotence—for 'without Me you can do nothing'—by a show of strength, by independence, or by criticising, complaining or abusing those who represent the Church. Teresa, on the other hand, although her writings are enlivened by caustic comments on her superiors and confessors, possessed a gift which made her write on one occasion: 'When I saw that my superior was resolved on this...I gave in at once, for Our Lord has granted me the favour of believing that my superiors are right in everything.'[24] This is an exceptional favour and, mercifully, an unnecessary one, against which I return to Abbot Marmion:

> Does this mean that we must give up our judgment so far as to make all the judgments of the Abbot our own? No. We cannot abdicate the light of our reason... Let us suppose that our reason...shows us things under an altogether different light ...we can then humbly expose to him our manner of looking at them; St Benedict, whose supernatural spirit is tempered by just such good sense, does not fail to suggest this to us... Again, is it that the abbot is infallible or possesses infused knowledge? Assuredly not. The graces of state which he has the right to expect from God do not go so far as to accord him this privilege. He can be mistaken, he is in fact mistaken at

---

[24] *Foundations*, in the Complete Works, trans. E. Allison Peers, London, 1950, Ch. 24, p. 123.

times; but the one who is never mistaken is the one who obeys.[25]

My own experience in community life is that when a person in authority is requiring obedience and looks most typically themselves, Mother X or Sister Y at their most fallible and human, all their well-known failings showing forth clearly, it is just then that God tests us. But if he sees that we are not deceived by appearances, but can see him behind that person at their least inspiring, he will bring good out of the situation in some unhoped-for way.

So far I have presented the case for obedience but, possibly because disobedience is the primal sin and therefore is the flaw at the heart of both the visible and invisible creation, obedience is not for most of us as clear-cut as I may be making it appear. On the other hand, neither is it as dangerous and as complex as some objections would have us believe. For instance, Nazi Germany is all too commonly held up as an example of the evils which follow from carrying out orders with absolute obedience. And indeed it is. But it is an example of the evils which follow from obeying the instincts of self-preservation, self-interest, greed and fear. Such obedience cannot, with any justification, be spoken about in the same breath as that which is wrought from the renunciation of temporal self-interest and self-will for the sake of the Church and the divine glory. This latter obedience is indeed a 'holy obedience', well described in the opening paragraph of the chapter on Obedience in our SLG Rule:

Obedience is the means whereby the human will is re-established in its true purpose to be one with the will of God. It must always be recognised as a free response of love and the means whereby the spirit of sacrifice may be more perfectly attained.

---

[25] Op. cit. (see n. 19), pp. 269–270.

Now that phrase, 'a free response of love', is absolutely crucial. If we obey because we are constrained to obey, out of fear or from self-interest, we can do ourselves more harm than in any other way. Each of us possesses an integrity which we must not on any account allow to be violated—whatever the immediate effect on our prospects might be—and we should be grateful that authority in the Church of England is not, normally speaking, exercised in such a way as to violate the individual conscience. (Violation of conscience is more likely to occur in the fringe religious groups which abound. Such groups derive part of their power from the desire, deep within many of us, to return to the state of primal innocence when all was obedience. But we cannot go back. We have to go forward with our lost innocence, and grapple in the depths of our own conscience with the problems of obedience as and when they arise.)

What we do meet in the Church of England, however, is a pressure to conform, and it is clear that this pressure is on the increase. But while you are unlikely to be forced to bow your will to a powerful bishop, you may feel constrained to remain silent at a deanery meeting, for example, when obedience to a higher law would give you the courage and freedom to speak out. But courage and freedom come only when there is nothing of self, nothing of the ego at work. And I can know this by a certain tranquillity in myself. But if I am trembling with rage or nerves, or whatever, then, however 'right' objectively I may be, it is certain that I am not sufficiently purified to perform the task I see needs to be done, or else God's moment has not arrived, or he has not chosen me to do it. On the other hand, the agitation may arise because temperamentally one is not the kind of person who speaks up against the consensus. If that is so in your case you must begin to practise in defiance of your temperament without delay! The Church needs bold, free spirits, who can think and speak courageously. But it also needs spirits who, having done so, peacefully leave the rest to God and are not dismayed or angry because the results in time and space are not immediately accomplished.

* * * * *

We believe in...all that is...unseen...

Earlier we were thinking about the primary act of disobedience and of how it opened the eyes of the senses, which until then had been shut, and shut the eyes of the spirit, which until then had been open. In the next stage of the story God enumerates to Adam and his wife the consequences to mankind of their disobedience; that, among other things, the pains of the woman in childbearing will be greatly multiplied, and that the man will eat bread in the sweat of his face. God then clothes them in 'tunics of skin'—the literal rendering of Genesis 3:21—that is to say, he gives them the kind of bodies in which they will now suffer these things. The Hebrew word for skin here, which is in the singular, applies to human as well as to animal skin, exactly as the word Eve, meaning 'living', the name by which Adam calls his wife in the previous verse, applies both to animal and human life (as against a nearly identical word which is used only in relation to humans).

All this suggests that an alteration of state has taken place in Adam and Eve and that they now inhabit bodies which are common in character to both animal and human creation—not, as has been generally assumed, that God slaughtered animals and processed their skins in order to provide them with clothes. Adam and Eve have, in any case, already shown, on first seeing they were naked (3:7), that they are capable of clothing themselves. No, the skin God now gives them is intrinsic to their fallen nature which, in the light of this reading, further suggests that whereas before their sin

47

Adam and Eve had enjoyed the benefits of incorporeality, now they are confined in corporeality—not, I think, as a punishment for their disobedience but as the ineluctable consequence of it (though the consequences of sin are always experienced by us as punishment).

This view of the text illuminates—for me, at least—the nature of Christ's incarnation, death and resurrection, for it would follow that Christ took upon himself precisely this 'tunic of skin' that, by his life of obedience in the garment of disobedience, and by his nailing of it to the cross, the body which God had created for the human race at the beginning might be restored to us—whence it becomes possible to understand what is meant by 'the resurrection of the body', which the appearances of Jesus after he had risen from the dead are at some pains to make clear to us.[26]

There is yet more to be gained from the Hebrew word for 'skin'. As a noun it consists of the same letters (*ayin, waw, resh*) as the verb 'to make blind', which the Hebrew dictionary specifically links with skin, giving 'whence blindness as cataract.' This verb in turn gives an adjective, usually used as a noun, 'the blind', and from this come the figurative meanings, 'the helpless', 'the groping', and also 'the dull, the unreceptive'. And does not that wonderfully describe our state in relation to all that is unseen? For, whatever our original state, whether or not we fell from it into a different one, and whatever it was we were clothed in when we fell, the fact of the matter is that, in relation to the invisible world we are—normally speaking—blind.

Now it is, it seems to me, precisely on account of this blindness in relation to the invisible world that God provides each one of us with a guardian angel, for 'he wills not the

---

[26] The view of Gen. 3:21 suggested here was subsequently developed by me in a paper, 'Spiritual Reading', published in the Winter 1990 issue of the *Fairacres Chronicle*, and again in *Wide as God's Love*, a collection of articles from the *Chronicle*, published by New City, 1994.

death of a sinner'. For without an invisible guide in the invisible realm how could we, blind as we are to that realm, be led safely from death to life? But God has blessed us in the provision of an angel as a blind person is blessed in the provision of a guide dog. And we have to learn to repose the same perfect trust in our angel as one who is blind learns to repose in his dog. We have all seen a blind person standing passively at the side of a sitting dog, waiting until the dog stands up and leads its charge across a road. And would we not be alarmed to see such a person, full of self-will, suddenly tugging impatiently at the dog and marching straight into the traffic? But that is how we must constantly appear to the heavenly host. So we have to learn to listen, to watch the signs, to be flexible, stopping when we want to go, and going when we should like to stop.

> Behold, I send an angel before thee,
> to keep thee in the way, and to bring thee
> into the place which I have prepared.
> Beware of him, and obey his voice.
> Exodus 23:20–21.

But, you may object, I do not hear his voice so how can I obey it? To which I would reply, You have heard his voice and you are obeying it or you would not be where you are, for it is your angel who has enabled you to respond thus far to God's purposes for you. So, go on, and listen ever more attentively to his promptings. They are, in contrast to the promptings of the demons, always very quiet and deceptively lacking in any sense of urgency so that obedience to them needs to be all the more prompt or you will, in a famous phrase, 'have missed the moment.'

This obedience to the promptings of the unseen world of God's messengers will become more necessary as you mature in your priestly ministry. For, as you become less and less under the immediate authority of human persons, you will need, through prayer and moments of recollection, to become more and more attuned to the authority of angelic persons if you are to be protected from error and misfortune. Only so will your ministry participate in that supernatural realm which the members of your flock, whether they are aware of it or not, will look to you to mediate to them. Therefore, may your citizenship increasingly be in heaven, from where, in the words of St Paul,

> we await a saviour, the Lord Jesus Christ,
> who will change the body of our humiliation
> to be like his glorious body,
> according to the operation of his ability
> to subject all things to himself.
>
> Philippians 3:20–21

*　*　*　*　*